THE SCRIBAL COMPANION

STUDENT WORKBOOK
(REVISED & EXPANDED EDITION)

THERESA HARVARD JOHNSON

ISBN-13: 978-1539754077

ISBN-10: 1539754073

Printed in the United States of America.
2016 Second Edition

"Study to shew thyself approved unto God, a workman that needeth not to be ashamed, rightly dividing the word of truth."

~ 2 Timothy 2:15

Table of Contents

Introduction 4

Purpose of this Workbook 4

Covenant Use: The Scribal Companion 5

Instructions for Personal Study 5

Part I: Foundation Building 8

Session I: Consider Your Creative Scribal Ministry 10

Session II. Scribes of Old 11

Session III: Present Day Scribes 18

Session IV: Scribes Instructed in the Kingdom of Heaven 21

Part II: Scribal Ministry 30

Session I. Publishing the News 32

Session II. Writing the Word of the Lord 34

Session III. Writing & Recording Prophetic Words 38

Part III. Transforming Your Ministry 42

Session I. Authentic Transformation 44

Session II: Your Gift Does Not Define You 46

Session III. The Purpose of Scribal Ministry 47

Session IV. Three Types of Christian Writers 52

Session V. Identifying Sheep, Goats & Wolves 52

Part IV: Breaking Spiritual Strongholds 56

Session I: Ministry Vs Entertainment 58

Session II: Motives & Motivation 65

Part V: Unleashing the Scribal Anointing 68

Session I: When Breakthrough Doesn't Come 70

Session II: A Foundation of Prayer 71

Session III. Unveiling the Power of Praise & Worship 73

Session IV. Unleashing The Scribal Anointing® Within 75

Introduction

For decades God's creative scribes have allowed Babylon, our world system, to define who they are as writers, journalists, poets, spoken word artists, novelists, playwrights, song writers, novelists, devotionalists, etc. in the body of Christ. The time has come to regain our identity – not by literary standards established through textbooks and prestigious literary circles – but by the word of God. It is only after learning who we are in Christ and applying that foundation to our lives that we can effectively operate in our gifts and talents and fulfill our scribal assignments on earth.

There is a definite place for skill in the worship arts **(1 Chronicles 15:22)**; but it is of more importance to have wisdom, knowledge and understanding in the realm of the spirit. It is more important to receive revelation from God's word and walk obediently in it. You see God values balance. The Apostle Paul explains this well in **Philippians 3**. He talks about how everything he learned with his carnal mind means nothing to him in comparison with what he has gained from Christ Jesus. *There is an imbalance in the operation of scribal gifts today.* The greater influence on scribes is coming from the world not God's word.

The Scribal Companion is a student workbook designed to walk hand-in-hand with the training and demonstration manual, *The Scribal Anointing*. Through self-study, it guides literary ministers through the scriptures, leading them into the depths of God's heart concerning their scribal destiny and purpose.

Purpose of this Workbook

The *Scribal Companion* was written specifically:

1. To assist you in building a scriptural foundation for your identity in Christ as a scribe;

2. To give you practice and practical training in searching the scriptures and researching relevant biblical historical facts to uncover what God is saying about the ministry he has entrusted to you;

3. To unveil God's original purpose and intent for scribal ministry in the earth;

4. To examine what it means to walk in a pure, uncompromising ministry that brings honor and glory singularly to God; and

5. To fortify the urgency and zeal for ministry in your heart through affirmation concerning your prophetic call to write.

Covenant Use: The Scribal Companion

The Scribal Anointing training and demonstration manual and *The Scribal Companion* are valuable tools to help individual writers achieve spiritual maturity in their scribal call to ministry. Please feel free to use them for personal study and enrichment.

Please note that leaders who have earned a Certificate to Teach through the Voices of Christ Apostolic-Prophetic School of the Scribe are authorized and encouraged to use *The Scribal Anointing as* an instruction manual and/or teaching tool for others. While others may choose to do so, please understand that they <u>are not</u> representing the School of the Scribe if they cannot produce an original teaching certificate. As a result, certain premises in our teaching could be grossly misinterpreted and conveyed if full understanding has not been presented to them from the heart of God in which *The Scribal Anointing* was written and the ministers trained through Voices of Christ have been taught. You are, however, encouraged to use this workbook as a study guide individually and with a community of scribes to explore and dig deeper in your calling. I pray that the integrity and the character of Christ continues to rest fully upon you.

Instructions for Personal Study

As you work your way through *The Scribal Companion*, begin each session of study with prayer. Ask the Lord to open your ears that you may hear and prepare your hearts to receive his divine revelation, instruction, direction and correction. Conclude your prayer by giving the Holy Spirit your will so that He can have his way in your heart; thereby enlarging your ministry in the spirit realm as well as the natural.

This book will transform your ministry.

I encourage you to begin your study using the King James Version of the bible. It is regarded as the most accurate translation of the scriptures from their original text to English. Many of the bible versions released today have "watered down" the word. So much so, that much of its original meaning has been lost. I implore you to be mindful of your study tools. Also, consider obtaining a copy of the Amplified Bible as well. It defines key terms in the scriptures based on their original meaning from Hebrew and Greek texts. I have used KJV and the AMP versions of the bible in *The Scribal Anointing*.

Although not required, I also recommend that you obtain a good "bible" dictionary, a biblical concordance and, perhaps, a book or two on Jewish culture – particularly as it relates to biblical history. Check out the bibliography and sources in the back of The Scribal Anointing book. Many questions in *The Scribal Companion* have scripture references that are intended to give you a *starting point* for study. They should encourage you to search the scriptures as you move through *The Scribal Anointing*. In addition, there are a number of exercises that focus on awakening and revealing the heart of the prophetic writer in you as well as your attitude, opinion and overall perspective concerning the word of God.

Finally, I encourage you to take your time. Please *do not* try to complete the entire workbook and study guide in one day. Take one step at a time. Meditate on what you have learned and allow the Holy Spirit to take you to higher heights and deeper depths in understanding. Also, fully answer the questions or complete the short essays as you go. Each session builds upon the last to bring you into a place of full understanding – even if these are things you already know.

God has a plan for you as a prophetic scribe. It is my prayer that the fullness of your ministry unto God comes forth in due season and that you are postured correctly to fulfill your destiny and purpose in Christ Jesus. Come, let us take this journey together!

Part I:
Foundation Building

"According to the grace of God which was given to me, as a wise master builder I have laid the foundation, and another builds on it. But let each one take heed how he builds on it. For no other foundation can anyone lay than that which is laid, which is Jesus Christ."
~1 Corinthians 3:10-11

Introduction: The foundation has been set with Jesus Christ. If he is indeed our personal "Lord" and "Savior" then we can only build upon *His* foundation with the tools *He* has released to us. Consider this for a moment. The average person spends nearly a third of their lives being indoctrinated in the world system. We attend elementary, middle and high schools; colleges and universities. We train for the workforce, and collect additional information from influences in our homes, communities, and through the media. By the time Christ is invited into their lives, our minds have already been constructed, clouded and corrupted by the world system. By the time we enter God's house, we often try to operate in the things of the spirit with that same "worldly" mind set. We tend to apply strategies and techniques from the world to facilitate the plans God has given. It does not work. Instead, God must lovingly renovate the mind. Tearing down those mindsets that are not like his until we come into the knowledge of "who we are" in Christ. Only then, can we begin building upon the foundation with the *right* tools for the job. Are you ready for an apostolic renovation?

Memory Scripture: 1 Corinthians 3:10-11

Session I: Consider Your Creative Scribal Ministry

1. **Describe Your Scribal Ministry**. Tell us when you began writing for the Lord. What were you doing and what inspired you?

   _____
   _____
   _____
   _____
   _____
   _____
   _____
   _____
   _____
   _____
   _____
   _____
   _____
   _____
   _____

2. **What is your writing trigger?** Are you inspired by dreams in the middle of the night? Are you inspired by sermons, nature, experiences or even people? Do you write in the midst of personal trials or joy? What triggers your prophet writing flow?

   _____
   _____
   _____
   _____
   _____
   _____

_____
_____

3. Have you felt compelled to share your writings with others? If so, in what way(s)?

_____
_____
_____
_____
_____

4. **How often do you write?** Do you believe writing is an integral part of who you are? If so, please explain?

_____
_____
_____
_____
_____

5. **What do you expect to learn about the scribal ministry through this study?** Write down your expectations now before digging in, and then after you study The Scribal Anointing®, come back and revisit what you've written.

_____
_____
_____
_____
_____

Session II. Scribes of Old
(Read & Review *The Scribal Anointing*®, pgs. 5-15.)

1. **What is a scribe?**

   a. My definition? (Before reading the book, The Scribal Anointing®.)

   _____
   _____
   _____

   b. The dictionary's definition?

   _____
   _____
   _____

c. The biblical definition? (After reading pages 9-14 of The Scribal Anointing®.)

_____
_____
_____

2. **Scribes who copied the Law of Moses (also called the Law and Torah), were called** _____, which means _____.

3. **According to Phillip R. Davis, scribes of antiquity were identified as** _____, _____, **and** _____ **in the ancient near east.**

4. **What have you learned about the type of discipline scribes demonstrated in the midst of their calling?** _____

_____
_____
_____
_____

5. **Name up to five roles scribes held during biblical times?** (Support your answer with scripture references.)
    a. _____
    b. _____
    c. _____
    d. _____
    e. _____

6. **Scribes took their roles in the temple and in the Kingdom very seriously.** What are some of the characteristics that reveal their devotion?
    a. _____
    b. _____
    c. _____
    d. _____
    e. _____
    f. _____

7. **What characteristics do you have as a scribe to the King that shows your devotion to scribal ministry?**

    a. _____

b. _____

c. _____

d. _____

e. _____

f. _____

8. **Scribes primarily served these two groups in the scriptures:** _____ **and** _____. Some were also _____ to write contracts, divorce decrees, marriage agreements, etc.

9. **A** _____ **is a scribe who drafted documents under the Priest or King's guidance, while a** _____ **was charged with making perfect hand written copies of the law.**

10. **What** *believer* **in the New Testament was a devout Pharisee who served faithfully until he was converted? Explain. (Acts 23)** _____

_____

_____

_____

_____

11. **Scribes originally served on the** _____, **an administrative council in the bible formed by God himself.** Moses was charged with choosing its ____ members. Of that number, approximately _____ were scribes.

12. **This council was made up of** _____, _____ **and** _____ **scribes.**

13. **How was the term "officer" understood in the Old Covenant as it relates to Numbers 11?** _____

_____

_____

_____

_____

14. **How were these leaders chosen? List the guidelines that God gave to Moses.**

_____

_____

_____

_____

_____
_____
_____

15. In your own words, what do these guidelines say about the character of these scribes and their level of accountability among the people? Is this still relevant today? Explain.

_____
_____
_____
_____
_____
_____
_____
_____
_____
_____
_____

16. Honestly, what godly character traits do you exhibit in considering the dedication of scribes of old? What areas can be improved in your life? Explain. _____

_____
_____
_____
_____
_____
_____
_____
_____
_____
_____

17. What role did this council serve in the body and in the kingdom? How does the role of the scribe relate to the local church today? (Numbers 11; 1 Corinthians 12:28; Exodus 18:13-26; Acts 6)

_____
_____
_____
_____
_____
_____
_____
_____
_____

18. List some additional characteristics of the scribes of old that stand out to you?

_____
_____
_____
_____
_____
_____
_____
_____
_____
_____
_____
_____

19. When you consider the reputation of biblical scribes, what is the first thing that comes to mind? Why?

_____
_____
_____
_____
_____

20. The reputation of scribes in Christian culture is negative for the most part. Explain why in your own words? (Matthew 12:4; Acts 4:5, 5:34, 6:12; Jeremiah 8:8)

_____
_____
_____
_____
_____
_____
_____
_____
_____
_____
_____
_____
_____
_____

21. Now that you have learned more about scribes of old, how has your perspective changed? _____

_____
_____
_____

_____
_____

22. How did scribes rise to power? Why were they esteemed among the people? (Numbers 3:27-32, 4:4-15, 7:9)

_____
_____
_____
_____
_____
_____
_____
_____
_____
_____

23. Some scribes were also members of competing political-religious groups. Name the two groups mentioned in *The Scribal Anointing®* and describe their distinctive characteristics? (Acts 23; Matthew 22; Mark 12)

_____
_____
_____
_____
_____
_____
_____
_____
_____
_____
_____
_____
_____
_____
_____

24. Jesus heavily rebuked scribes in Matthew 23. List at least six characteristics that angered Christ.

    a. _____
    b. _____
    c. _____
    d. _____
    e. _____
    f. _____

25. With Holy Spirit as your guide, seriously consider whether or not you have walked in any of the ungodly strongholds associated with the scribes of old. Write your response here.

_____
_____
_____
_____
_____
_____
_____
_____
_____
_____
_____

26. Why did Jesus tell the people to do as the "scribes and Pharisees" instructed but do not follow their example for living in Matthew 23. Is this still true today? Explain.

_____
_____
_____
_____
_____
_____
_____

27. Scribes who held the title "scribe" were not random people who loved to write. They were professionals trained and appointed to their positions. Name at least four professional scribes from the scriptures and describe their "job responsibilities." Using the *Chart of Biblical Scribes* in *The Scribal Anointing*, search the scriptures.

_____
_____
_____
_____
_____
_____
_____

28. What is the first ministry of the scribe? _____

29. In what ways were scribes considered masters in the midst of the community?

_____
_____
_____

_____

_____

30. In addition to being teachers and interpreters of the word, scribes were also _____ of the word? Explain how they fulfilled their ministry. _____

_____

_____

_____

_____

_____

_____

Session III: Present Day Scribes
(Read & Review *The Scribal Anointing*®, pgs. 31-52.)

1. Highlight the similarities and differences between scribes of old and scribes today based on what you've learned, and what you've observed?

_____

_____

_____

_____

_____

_____

2. In your own words, explain why we are not scribes of old? _____

_____

_____

_____

_____

_____

3. What supernatural move of the spirit gave birth to the ministry of the "present day" scribe? Explain.

_____

_____

_____

_____

_____

_____

_____

_____

4. **In what way does Acts 2 impact the ministry of the prophetic scribe?**

_____

_____

_____

_____

_____

5. **Why is it important for Christians to distinguish between the "scribe of old" and a "present day" scribe?**

_____

_____

_____

_____

_____

_____

_____

_____

6. **Some people do not believe that all men have access to the gift of prophecy. Is this true? What does the bible teach about this?** (Acts 2:1-4, 17-21)

_____

_____

_____

_____

_____

_____

_____

_____

_____

7. **What is the purpose of prophecy and why are we encouraged to "desire" to prophesy?** (1 Corinthians 14:39)

_____

_____

_____

_____

_____

_____

_____

_____

_____

_____

8. **Do you believe that the Lord speaks prophetically through you? If so, discuss your experiences.**

_____

_____

_____

_____

_____

_____

_____

9. **Review *The Emergence of Scribal Ministry* chart (pg. 35) and exam the role of scribes of old verses present day scribes.** Do you see the scribal progression? Do you recognize yourself or others scribes that you know in any of these areas?

_____

_____

_____

_____

_____

_____

_____

10. **Identify the three levels of prophetic writing and scribal ministry?**

_____

_____

_____

_____

_____

_____

_____

_____

_____

11. **Quickly turn back to The Emergence of Scribal Ministry chart (pg. 35).** Can you identify those scribal roles in one or more of the "three levels" identified? You can use a separate sheet of paper to do this or use the space provided below. _____

_____

_____

_____

_____

_____

_____

_____

_____

_____

_____

_____

_____

_____

_____

12. There are 10 reasons why God has called us to write. After reviewing and studying each one of them, identify the area or areas that speaks to your prophetic writing gift? (Pgs. 38-41)

_____

_____

_____

_____

_____

_____

_____

_____

_____

Session IV: Scribes Instructed in the Kingdom of Heaven

(Read & Review *The Scribal Anointing*®, pgs. 43-52.)

1. What biblical patriarch is the example for scribal ministry today? Explain why?

_____

_____

_____

_____

_____

_____

2. Why is this patriarch so revered in biblical history – particularly in this area of ministry?

_____

_____

_____

_____

_____

_____

3. **Why was Ezra called a scribe instructed in the Kingdom of God?** What is about his life that caused him to stand out before the Lord?

_____

_____

_____

_____

_____

_____

_____

4. **What lessons can you take away from the scribal ministry of Ezra and apply to your life and ministry today?**

_____

_____

_____

_____

_____

_____

_____

5. **Define the Ezra Pattern.** _____

_____

_____

_____

_____

_____

_____

6. **What role will the Ezra Pattern play in your life as a scribe from this point forward?** _____

_____

_____

_____

_____

_____

7. **Why did Jesus Christ speak to his disciples in parables? How does this apply to you today as a prophetic scribe?**

_____

_____

_____

_____

_____
_____

8. In your own words, explain the critical significance of the revelation hidden in Matthew 13:52 to the life of a scribe? Point out the areas that stand out most to you.

_____
_____
_____
_____
_____
_____

9. How does the revelation of *The Scribal Anointing*® relate to the ministry of Ezra?

_____
_____
_____
_____
_____
_____

10. Take some time to review this key phrase from Matthew 13:52, "master of his house?" How does this apply to you personally? What is Jesus saying?

_____
_____
_____
_____
_____
_____

11. In your own words, define *The Scribal Anointing*®?

_____
_____
_____
_____
_____
_____
_____
_____
_____

12. **Why did God describe Ezra as a scribe instructed in the Kingdom of Heaven?** (Ezra 7)

_____
_____
_____
_____
_____
_____
_____

13. **There are six characteristics Ezra had as a priest and a scribe in the scriptures. Study each characteristic and summarize how they differ from the scribes who were rebuked in the scriptures.** (Ezra 7-8; Matthew 23)

_____
_____
_____
_____
_____
_____
_____
_____
_____
_____
_____
_____
_____
_____

14. **How does Matthew 13:52 compare to God's description of Ezra in Ezra 7:12; Ezra 7:21?**

_____
_____
_____
_____
_____
_____
_____
_____
_____
_____
_____
_____
_____
_____

15. Review the steps Ezra took to maintain his right standing with God in detail in *The Scribal Anointing*®. Key elements from each of the items are displayed in the chart below. On a scale of one to 10 rate yourself and note any areas revealed by Holy Spirit in which you need to come up.

Ezra's Path To Right Standing	My Path To Right Standing
Rooted in the word of God (2 Timothy 2:15)	
Heard and obeyed God's voice (1 Samuel 15:22)	
Prepared his heart to receive instructions from God (James 1:23-25)	
King and Priest (Revelations 5:10; 1 Corinthians 12:27-29)	
Blessed the Lord and thanked him consistently (Psalm 93:1-3; Ephesians 1:15-16; Psalm 100)	
Fast and pray for humility (Ezra 8:21-23)	
Do all that is required of you by God. (Ezra 7:21-22)	

16. **Take an inventory of your scribal ministry before proceeding further into this study.** Set aside time for meditation and prayer. Ask yourself this question in the presence of Holy Spirit: Does my life exemplify the ministry Christ referred to here? Am I on the path that leads to righteousness? (Instead of answering this here, write your response in your journal.)

17. **List some characteristics of people who write as a hobby?**

_____
_____
_____
_____
_____
_____
_____

18. **List some characteristics of people who write because they love writing?**

_____
_____
_____
_____
_____
_____
_____

19. **Are all Christian writer's prophetic scribes? Why or why not?**

_____
_____
_____

20. **Define passion? How do you exemplify the passion in your life for your scribal ministry?**

_____
_____
_____

21. **What is urgency from a biblical perspective?**

_____
_____
_____

22. What is urgency from a world perspective?

_____

_____

_____

23. Why do we need the God kind of urgency operating in our lives?

_____

_____

_____

24. Can you recall instances in which you've walked in the God kind of urgency? What about the world's type of urgency?

_____

_____

_____

_____

_____

_____

_____

_____

25. Define passion. Discuss the role passion plays in your life.

_____

_____

_____

_____

_____

_____

26. How is a person equipped with passion, urgency and zeal?

_____

_____

_____

_____

_____

_____

27. Name three biblical figures other than Jesus who exemplified passion, zeal and urgency in their ministry. Give examples of how they proved themselves to be true to the faith.

a. _____
_____
_____

b. _____
_____
_____

c. _____
_____
_____

Part II: Scribal Ministry

*"The secret things belong unto the Lord our God:
but those things which are revealed belong to us and
to our children forever, that we may do all the words of the Law."*
~Deuteronomy 29:29

Introduction: Revelation. God wants us to live in the spiritual realm where the revelation concerning the secret things in His word are revealed to us daily. Anyone can read information and follow the instructions provided. It is only when the information we receive becomes revelatory to us that it has a deeper meaning and the potential to transform our lives. It is that point that information becomes more than just instructions or directions. It becomes a part of our value system and character. It is here that God *fortifies* his relationship with us and we move into a place of intimacy with him. It is here that we become *concerned* with what is pleasing to God and we reject what is pleasing to man. Where do you stand in your walk with God? Does pleasing him matter to you? Make a decision today to follow God and mean it. What you do is not just affecting you but the generations who will follow the legacy you leave behind.

Memory Scripture: Deuteronomy 29:29

Session I. Publishing the News
(Read & Review *The Scribal Anointing*, pgs. 55-58.)

1. **Define publishing.**

   a. My definition.

   _____
   _____
   _____

   b. The dictionary's definition.

   _____
   _____
   _____

   c. The biblical definition.

   _____
   _____
   _____

2. **Where is the first mention of the word "publish" in the bible?** What were the circumstances that led Moses to make this declaration before the people?

   _____
   _____
   _____
   _____
   _____
   _____

3. **Is what Moses said a statement that we can declare before the people around us today?** Why or why not?

_____
_____
_____
_____
_____
_____

4. **Why is it important to use the original meaning of words (as interpreted in Hebrew culture) in the scriptures verses the meaning of words in a regular dictionary?**

_____
_____
_____
_____
_____
_____

5. **Ignorance breeds _____; but _____ births success.** In your own words, explain what this means. Cite scriptures.

_____
_____
_____
_____
_____

6. **Read Luke 12:47-49 in the KJV and then the AMP version of the bible.** In your own words, please explain why there is no excuse for disobedience among believers in the eyes of God?

_____
_____
_____
_____
_____

7. **Name at least five different ways God has commanded us to publish the gospel?**

    a. _____
    b. _____
    c. _____
    d. _____
    e. _____

8. **Choose at least one bible verse that includes the word "publish" or a variation of it.** Using the Hebrew and Greek definitions, replace the word publish with each one of those definitions to get the full understanding of what the word of God is saying.

_____
_____
_____
_____
_____

9. **Is publishing solely dependent on releasing words in print in the eyes of the Lord?** If not, what is the greater responsibility?

_____
_____
_____
_____
_____

10. **Read Ecclesiastes 12:11-13.** What is meant by this scripture: "Of making many books there is no end."

_____
_____
_____
_____
_____

11. **Do we have a greater opportunity to *publish* the gospel today than the scribes did thousands of years ago?** Explain.

_____
_____
_____
_____
_____
_____

Session II. Writing the Word of the Lord
(Read & Review *The Scribal Anointing*, pgs. 59-64.)

1. **Define prophetic.**

_____
_____

2. **Define prophecy.**

_____

_____

_____

_____

_____

3. **What is the gift of prophecy?**

_____

_____

_____

_____

_____

_____

_____

_____

4. **What is a prophetic scribe?**

_____

_____

_____

_____

_____

_____

5. **What is the purpose of the "gift of prophecy" in the body of Christ?** (1 Corinthians 12; Acts 2)

_____

_____

_____

_____

_____

_____

_____

6. **Is there a different manifestation of the gift of prophetic writing in the lives of apostles and prophets? Explain.**

_____

_____

_____

_____

_____

_____

_____

_____
_____
_____
_____
_____
_____

7. **What is a skilled writer? In your own words, provide an example.**

_____
_____
_____
_____
_____
_____
_____
_____
_____

8. **A skilled writer focuses on:**
    a. _____
    b. _____
    c. _____
    d. _____

9. **What is a prophetic writer or a prophetic scribe?** In your own words, provide an example.

_____
_____
_____
_____
_____
_____
_____
_____
_____

10. **A prophetic writer or a prophetic scribe focuses exclusively on:**
    a. _____
    b. _____

11. **What does a prophetic scribe base their worth or merit on?**

_____
_____
_____
_____
_____
_____
_____
_____

12. **In reflecting on where you are right now in your walk with the Lord, has your emphasis been on your ability or skill; or on the desire to accurately hear the voices of the Lord?**

_____
_____
_____
_____
_____

13. **In your spare time, I want to challenge you to look at how "writing is taught" in a university setting.** You can do this simply by researching fine arts curriculums or studies in writing on the Internet. The course descriptions will indicate their focus. As you read them, explain how this differs from a focus on the spiritual things. You may do this in your journal.

14. **What are some of the characteristics a prophetic scribe *must* have?** Does this remind you of Ezra? If so, in what ways.

_____
_____
_____
_____
_____
_____
_____
_____

15. **What is a seasoned scribe?**

_____
_____
_____
_____

16. What strongholds does the skilled scribe face? How should they be broken?

_____

_____

_____

_____

_____

_____

_____

_____

_____

_____

17. What separates a prophetic scribe from a skilled writer in the sense discussed here?

_____

_____

_____

_____

_____

_____

_____

_____

_____

_____

18. Read Proverbs 16:1-4. Explain why it is important to commit our works to the Lord.

_____

_____

_____

_____

_____

_____

_____

_____

Session III. Writing & Recording Prophetic Words
(Read & Review *The Scribal Anointing*, pgs. 69-73.)

1. **How you write or record prophecy is specifically associated with your own unique _____.**

2. **Prophetic words can take on numerous forms. What are some of those forms?**

_____

_____

_____
_____

3. If you write or record prophetic words, what form or forms does the prophetic word take within your own ministry?

_____
_____
_____

4. Why is character important to prophecy? Take some time to study out passages of scripture in the Bible that talks about the character (1 Corinthians 13:1-3, Romans 5:3-5, Galatians 5:22-23). Honestly discuss where you stand in your character toward God and others. _____

_____
_____
_____
_____
_____
_____
_____
_____

5. Read Ephesians 4 in its entirety. What does it mean to administer the Ephesians 4:11 ministry in love as you understand it?

_____
_____
_____
_____
_____
_____
_____

6. Highlight the three foundational keys to writing and recording prophecy? _____

_____
_____
_____
_____
_____
_____
_____
_____

7. **Why are these keys significant as you see it?**

_____
_____
_____
_____
_____
_____
_____
_____
_____

8. **Review the recommended guidelines on writing and recording prophecy. Pick two or three that you consider important and explain why.** _____

_____
_____
_____
_____
_____
_____
_____
_____
_____

9. **Why is knowing the Word of God critical to writing and recording prophecy?** _____

_____
_____
_____
_____
_____
_____
_____
_____
_____

10. **What is God's mission? Why is this significant?** _____

_____
_____
_____
_____
_____
_____
_____
_____
_____

11. **God's word always gives _____.**

Session IV: Is God Speaking
(Read The Scribal Anointing, pgs. 73-74)

1. **How do you know that God is speaking in your writing verses you speaking from your own soul?**

   _____
   _____
   _____
   _____
   _____
   _____

2. **How have you identified the voice of God in your own life up until this point?** Has it been through your pastor, your mentors as well as your personal study? What brings you confirmation?

   _____
   _____
   _____
   _____
   _____

3. **When God is speaking, what will His word always do?**

   _____
   _____
   _____

4. **When God speaks, he produces life.** In your writings, are the words penned on your computer screen and inside your notebooks life-giving words that mirror the heart and mind of God?

5. **If the word of God is not _____, then the word of God cannot _____.**

6. **What are the keys to accurately hearing and discerning God's voice? Studying the bible is one. Name two others: _____ and _____.**

7. **Using the scriptures, list at least four ways that Father speaks to us:**
_____, _____, _____ **and**
_____.

8. **Take a close look at the lives of one or more biblical figures:** Abraham, Isaac, Jacob, Isaiah, Moses, Esther, Deborah, Peter, Paul, etc. Choose one of them and explain at least one method God used to speak to them. Tell us why or how they knew it was the voice of God that they heard. Also, look at examples of their disobedience to God and review the circumstances.

9. **Take a close look at the lives of one or more biblical figures:** Abraham, Isaac, Jacob, Isaiah, Moses, Esther, Deborah, Peter, Paul, etc. Choose one of them and explain at least one method God used to speak to them. Tell us why or how they knew it was the voice of God that they heard. Also, look at examples of their disobedience to God and review the circumstances. _____

_____
_____
_____
_____
_____
_____

In your journal, share one of the most memorable and profound moments when the Lord spoke to you and you clearly recognized His voice.

Part III. Transforming Your Ministry

Session I. Authentic Transformation

(Read & Review The Scribal Anointing®, pgs. 77-90)

Introduction: Father is calling his prophetic scribes to move out of the world system and completely into the Kingdom of Heaven. No longer are we to establish what we are doing by standards outside of the will of God. This process takes time. In Jeremiah 29, the last of the exiles from Israel were sent into Babylon. They were given specific instructions by the prophet Jeremiah concerning how to live. In short, they were told to build their families and make their way prosperous using only the tools they'd been given by God. For 70 years, they were to do everything exactly the way the Lord had instructed them. Then, at the end of that period the Lord would fulfill the promises he had made concerning them. Obviously, when reading this chapter from a human perspective, the average person would see these requirements as overwhelming – especially the adults or leaders who knew that – in 70 years – they would be deceased. But in this, the Lord was showing us that in the Kingdom of Heaven "time" has a different and far deeper meaning. It also shows us that we are not only "doing our thing" but we are building for the future generations. So this place of transformation is really a place of spiritual growth, maturity and obedience. It is the putting on the mind of Christ in ways that we've never done before.

Memory Scripture: 1 Corinthians 2:13-16

1. **What are the first three steps involved in transforming your ministry?**

_____
_____
_____
_____
_____
_____
_____
_____
_____
_____

2. **Review each of these steps. Describe where you are in your relationship with God in each area of the transformation process.**

_____
_____
_____
_____
_____
_____
_____
_____
_____
_____

3. **The greatest obstacle prophetic writers face today is:**

_____
_____
_____
_____

4. **Explain the importance of being led by God in your writing verses perfecting writing techniques?**

_____
_____
_____
_____
_____
_____
_____
_____
_____
_____
_____
_____
_____
_____

5. **Why is it important to have a strong understanding of God's word of God?** (John 7:17; John 7:16; Romans 12:12)

_____
_____
_____
_____
_____

6. **How can focusing on the things you learned in the world place you off-balance concerning the things of God?** Now consider how they can complement one another.

_____
_____
_____
_____
_____

7. **The word of God** _____ **if the word of God** _____ .

8. **Why is building a "personal" relationship the God the most important aspect of your scribal ministry?** _____

   _____
   _____
   _____
   _____

9. **What are the advantages of having an active prayer life?** (Matthew 18:19-20; Psalm 4:3; Proverbs 15:29; John 9:31; Psalm 40:1)

   _____
   _____
   _____
   _____

10. **Why does God value the gathering of saints in a local church?** What does it mean to be accountable? (Romans 10:14; Jeremiah 3:15; Hebrews 10:24-25; James 5:16)

    _____
    _____
    _____
    _____
    _____
    _____

Session II: Your Gift Does Not Define You
(Read & Review *The Scribal Anointing*, pgs. 81-82)

1. **If you had the opportunity to introduce yourself to someone right now, how would you do it?** In fact, write your introduction.

   _____
   _____
   _____
   _____
   _____
   _____

2. **Have you always introduced yourself this way?** Explain.

   _____
   _____
   _____

_____
_____
_____

3. **What did Jesus base his identity upon?** How did he introduce himself? (Matthew 16:13-20)

_____
_____
_____
_____
_____
_____
_____
_____
_____
_____

4. **Why do you feel a need to share your scribal ministry with others?** Explain. (2 Corinthians 5:12-17)

_____
_____
_____
_____
_____

5. **How can a person worship their "gift" instead of worshipping God?** Share some examples from your own experiences.

_____
_____
_____
_____
_____

Session III. The Purpose of Scribal Ministry

(Read & Review *The Scribal Anointing*, pgs. 83-86)

1. **What does the word minister mean?**

   a. Your definition:

_____
_____
_____

b. The dictionary's definition:

_____
_____
_____

c. The biblical definition.

_____
_____
_____

2. **Our level of "service to others" increase with every spiritual promotion as well as with every natural promotion.** For example, in the natural sense a person who is a general employee is accountable only to his supervisor or director. When that person is promoted to a supervisory position, he is now responsible for directing those under him and he is accountable to producing results for the director above him. His level of responsibility has increased. The same is true for promotion in spiritual things. Those who have a greater level of wisdom and understanding also have a greater level of responsibility to others and accountability to God. What characteristics and examples can you identity from Christ's life that causes him to be more of a "servant" at his greatest promotion than he was before walking into his calling? *(Matthew, Mark, Luke & John)*

_____
_____
_____
_____
_____
_____
_____
_____
_____
_____
_____
_____
_____
_____

3. **How do these examples apply to you? Has your level of "service to others" increased?**

_____
_____
_____
_____
_____
_____
_____

4. **What does it really mean to "serve" others?** Consider this from a spiritual and a natural perspective. **(1 Peter 1:22, 4:8; 1 Corinthians 13:4-7; Matthew 20:26-28; Matthew 25:35-40; Luke 22:25-27; 2 Corinthians 5:17-19)**

_____
_____
_____
_____
_____
_____
_____
_____
_____
_____

5. **Of all the reasons we can site that Christ came from heaven to earth, what reason stands out far above the others in the scriptures to you?** Why?

_____
_____
_____
_____
_____
_____

6. **What ministry have ALL believers been given?** Why is it significant to your walk with the Lord and your scribal ministry?

_____
_____
_____
_____
_____
_____

7. **When you share your scribal ministry with others, what results are you looking for?**

_____
_____

_____
_____
_____
_____
_____

8. Pure ministry can be defined as when a believer uses "whatever gift he has been given" to earnestly share the gospel with others so that they might be saved. It's ministry that goes forth with the motives of God's heart – not the heart of man. **How have you exemplified this in your walk with God?**

_____
_____
_____
_____
_____

9. **Is your scribal ministry important to the body of Christ?** Explain.

_____
_____
_____
_____
_____

10. **Is your scribal ministry important to you?** Explain.

_____
_____
_____
_____
_____

11. **What do the scriptures say about "the value" of each person in the body of Christ?** Is any man "greater than you" in the eyes of God? Explain. (1 Corinthians 12)

_____
_____
_____
_____
_____

12. **The bible says that those members in the body of Christ who others deem to be less** honorable, on these _____.

13. **Based on the previous question, how can you show the love of God to those the world "deems" to be less honorable?**

_____

_____

_____

_____

_____

14. **What are the characteristics of men and women of God who have been "deemed as less honorable?"**

_____

_____

_____

_____

_____

15. **1 Samuel 16:7 says that man looks at the outward appearance,** but the Lord

_____.

16. **Do you believe your destiny and purpose is tied to the gifts that have placed in you?** Explain.

_____

_____

_____

_____

_____

17. **What could happen if you choose not to walk out your scribal ministry the way the Lord intended?**

_____

_____

_____

_____

_____

_____

_____

_____

_____

_____

Session IV. Three Types of Christian Writers
(Read & Review *The Scribal Anointing*, pg. 87-88)

1. **There are three types of Christian writers among the body today.** Looking at the descriptions provided, provide examples of books and/or writings that might fall in each categories. Take the time to look at the writings of popular Christian authors.

    a. _____
       _____
       _____
       _____
       _____

    b. _____
       _____
       _____
       _____
       _____
       _____

    c. _____
       _____
       _____
       _____
       _____
       _____

2. **With Holy Spirit guiding you, earnestly ask yourself what type of Christian writer you are – in this current place of your ministry?**

    _____
    _____
    _____
    _____
    _____
    _____
    _____
    _____
    _____
    _____

Session V. Identifying Sheep, Goats & Wolves
(Read & Review *The Scribal Anointing*, 88-90)

1. **What is the difference between sheep, goats and wolves? Answer in your own words.**

    _____
    _____
    _____

_____
_____
_____
_____

2. **As sheep what is expected of us? Consider Matthew 25:32-33, Matthew 28:18-20 and 2 Corinthians 5:18).**

_____
_____
_____
_____

3. **What type of fruit would follow the ministry of a sheep? Consider Ezra's ministry.**

_____
_____
_____

4. **What impact could a goat have in the midst of "scribal ministry?" How could the people around them suffer?**

_____
_____
_____
_____

5. **What are some of the characteristics of a goat?**

_____
_____
_____

6. **What is a wolf as described in the scriptures?** Explain in your own words.

_____
_____
_____

7. **How might a wolf operate in scribal ministry? What about a goat?**

_____
_____
_____
_____
_____

8. **As a believer, how can you identify a wolf?**

    _____
    _____
    _____
    _____

9. **Can a believer serve man and God?** Why or why not? Explain. (Matthew 6:24. 16:27; Romans 13:1-7; 1 John 2:15; Titus 1:16) _____

    _____
    _____
    _____
    _____

Part IV: Breaking Spiritual Strongholds

*"Now these are the ones sown among thorns; they are the ones who
hear the word, and the cares of this world, the deceitfulness of riches,
and the desires for other things entering in choke the word, and it becomes unfruitful."
--Mark 4:18, 19*

Session I: Ministry Vs Entertainment
(Read & Review *The Scribal Anointing*, pgs. 93-106)

The church today has become an entertainment Mecca. People are being lured into services and activities under the guise of evangelism; and in turn, the ministers and leaders who lure them are competing to keep those same people pleased and entertained. In the process, those who are "coming to Christ" in the midst of this chaos are learning to have church on a level that is completely outside of the will of God. Instead of being equipped to follow Christ, they are being equipped to satisfy the flesh and seek a "celebrity" type of Christ. In short, the world system has taken root in the sanctuary and Jezebel has set up her throne right next to the pulpit. This isn't just about a church building, but it's about your own temple as well. Is Jezebel sitting in your house? Have you become best friends with Ahab? Are the things of this world hard for you to release and you find yourself standing – ashamed of the purity of the gospel? This may sound harsh – but it is a reality for many. As you move through this study, consider the condition of *your heart* concerning God and examine the picture that has been painted in *your mind* about ministry. I pray that you allow the Holy Spirit to uncover God's will for your life and your scribal destiny.

Meditation Scriptures: Proverbs 19:21 & Luke 16:15

1. **Who is the lord (godhead/ruler) and master (captain/authority) of your life?** Study the scripture references, and answer this question honestly. (John 14:23-24; James 1:22-27)

   _____
   _____
   _____
   _____
   _____
   _____

2. **Define the word minister.**

   a. Your meaning

   _____
   _____

   b. Dictionary Meaning

   _____
   _____

   c. Biblical Meaning (Hebrew/Greek)

   _____
   _____

3. **Define the word ministry.**

   a. Your meaning

   _____
   _____

   b. Dictionary Meaning

   _____
   _____

   c. Biblical Meaning (Hebrew/Greek)

   _____
   _____

4. **List the four areas of ministry as defined by its Greek definition.** Then explain how you "publicly" and "privately" demonstrate each area of this type of ministry in your life.

   a. _____
      _____
      _____

   b. _____
      _____
      _____

   c. _____
      _____
      _____

5. **One of the most important areas of ministry is self-sacrifice or serving others at your "own expense."** How have you exemplified this in your life? Consider Esther, Jesus and the Apostle Paul. Then explain how this has crossed over into your "scribal ministry"? (Luke 22:7; Matthew 20:26-27; Matthew 25:40; John 15:13)

   _____
   _____
   _____
   _____
   _____
   _____
   _____
   _____

6. **Now, I want you to consider others who are or have been active in your life that exemplified self-sacrifice.** Please consider people in your personal sphere of influence. (1 John 3:14)

_____

_____

_____

_____

_____

_____

_____

7. **Is ministry an organization, corporation, conglomerate, a building or another tangible "thing" that you can touch or is it a lifestyle?** Explain the difference.

_____

_____

_____

_____

_____

_____

_____

8. **How has God instructed mankind to preach the gospel?** (2 Timothy 4:1-5) Is this approach for everyone or just for some people? Explain.

_____

_____

_____

_____

_____

_____

_____

9. **Review the Ezra Pattern again.** On a separate sheet of paper, go through each one of those points and explain how the light of God shines through your ministry. Share your strengths and weaknesses as they Holy Spirit leads. *(Allow yourself some time to complete this assignment, and listen to the voice of God on the inside of you.)*

10. **In your own words, define entertainment?**

_____

_____

_____

_____
_____

11. Define entertainment according to a Standard English dictionary. List at least 10 synonyms.

_____
_____
_____
_____
_____

12. The Greek origin of the biblical term entertain is XENIZO. It means to be

_____
_____

13. Find at least four examples of biblical entertainment/hospitality shown in the bible. One example is the parable of the Good Samaritan? (Luke 10:25-37)

_____
_____
_____
_____
_____

14. What makes "entertainment" defined by world standards ungodly?

_____
_____
_____
_____
_____
_____
_____

15. What relationship should believers have with unbelievers from the perspective of biblical entertainment and ministry? Consider the true biblical meaning of ministry and entertainment prior to answering.

_____
_____
_____
_____

16. List four characteristics of a minister of the gospel? Explain how you do or plan to exemplify these characteristics in your ministry.

a. _____
_____
_____

b. _____
_____
_____

c. _____
_____
_____

d. _____
_____
_____

17. List four characteristics of a world-focused entertainer? Explain how, if applicable, this type of approach to the gospel taints the gospel message.

○ _____
_____
_____

○ _____
_____
_____

○ _____
_____
_____

○ _____
_____
_____

18. What is it that you want to see happen in the lives of others as a result of your scribal ministry?

_____
_____
_____
_____

19. What do you love about your scribal ministry? Why?

_____
_____
_____
_____
_____

20. Are you a friend of the world or a friend of God? (James 4:4-7)

_____
_____
_____
_____
_____

21. What do the scriptures say about making alliances or agreements with the world-system? (Luke 16:13; James 4:4-7)

_____
_____
_____
_____
_____

22. What is highly valued among men is _____.

23. What do you value? Seriously consider this question.

24. Would God host a gospel showdown, talent search, or a competition in heaven using his "His" gifts? Why or why not?

_____
_____
_____
_____
_____
_____
_____
_____
_____
_____

25. Entertainment pleases _____. A person who entertains is constantly being placed in a position to _____

_____

26. What is competition?

_____
_____
_____
_____
_____
_____
_____
_____
_____
_____

27. Why is competition displeasing to the Lord?

_____
_____
_____
_____
_____
_____
_____
_____

28. In your own words, describe comparison.

_____
_____
_____
_____
_____
_____

29. The heart of every ministry should be rooted in _____ **in Jesus Christ. Explain why this is the root of everything we do.**

_____
_____
_____
_____
_____
_____
_____

_____
_____

Session II: Motives & Motivation
(Read *The Scribal Anointing,* pgs. 104-106)

1. **What does the word motive mean?**

    _____
    _____
    _____

2. **When looking at the life of Christ, what was His motive behind going the cross?** What was David's motive in writing psalms and music to the Lord?

    _____
    _____
    _____
    _____

3. **What was Lucifer's motive in attempting to take possession of the Kingdom of God?**

    _____
    _____
    _____
    _____

4. **Why is renewing our mind in the mind of Christ so important?**

    _____
    _____
    _____

5. **What role does reading your word and praying play in keeping motives pure?**

    _____
    _____
    _____
    _____

6. **Write a letter to God about your desire to walk in "pure" ministry. Share your heart with him and ask him to help you in any areas where you need assistance.**

    _____
    _____
    _____

Part V: Unleashing the Scribal Anointing

"And when they had laid many stripes on them, they threw them into prison, commanding the jailer to keep them securely. Having received such a charge, he put them into the inner prison and fastened their feet in the stocks.

But at midnight Paul and Silas were praying and singing hymns to God, and the prisoners were listening to them. Suddenly there was a great earthquake, so that the foundations of the prison were shaken; and immediately all the doors were opened and everyone's chains were loosed."
~ Acts 16:23-26

Session I: When Breakthrough Doesn't Come
(Read & Review *The Scribal Anointing*, pgs. 109-111)

1. **The greatest hindrance to truth in the body of Christ is _____. Explain.**

   _____
   _____
   _____
   _____
   _____
   _____

2. **In your own words, define ignorance?**

   _____
   _____
   _____
   _____
   _____
   _____

3. **What are strongholds?**

   _____
   _____
   _____
   _____
   _____
   _____

4. **In reviewing the things we've discussed in this book, what are some of the primary strongholds facing scribes today?**

   _____
   _____
   _____
   _____
   _____
   _____

5. **Ask Holy Spirit to reveal any strongholds in your life that may be preventing you from reaching your maximum potential in your scribal ministry?** Record what Father shows and/or instructs you to do in your journal.

6. **What is breakthrough?**

_____
_____
_____
_____
_____
_____

Session II: A Foundation of Prayer
(Read & Review *The Scribal Anointing*, pgs. 111-114)

1. **What role does prayer play in your life?**

_____
_____
_____
_____
_____
_____

2. **Why is prayer so important in the life of a prophetic scribe?**

_____
_____
_____
_____
_____
_____

3. **How does a person build a prayer life?**

_____
_____
_____
_____
_____
_____

4. **What are the effects of failing to build a prayer life?**

_____
_____
_____
_____
_____
_____

_____
_____

5. **What type of impact has prayer had in your life – even prayers from others?**

_____
_____
_____
_____
_____
_____

6. **Ministry birth outside of prayer is nothing more than a _____ .**

7. **Have you tried to walk out a "good idea" verses an idea inspired by Holy Spirit? If so, what did you learn?**

_____
_____
_____
_____
_____
_____

8. **Why is the ministry of prayer overlooked by so many of God's people? Share your thoughts on this issue.**

_____
_____
_____
_____
_____
_____

9. **Why is intercession important in the midst of scribal ministry?**

_____
_____
_____
_____
_____

10. **There can be no _____ of a godly anointing for _____ , _____ and _____ without intercession.**

11. Where there is _____ _____ there is _____ _____.

12. **Take some time, and ask Holy Spirit to (1) Teach you to pray for yourself; (2) Teach you to pray for your ministry; and (3) Teach you to pray for others.** Even if you already believe you have a strong prayer life, ask Him anyway and give Him the freedom to lead you into that area of prayer where you need revival. Sometimes we pray what we want, and don't often allow the Lord to lead us. Write what He reveals in your journal.

13. **Why does the Lord desire our HOUSES (physical body, ministry and places where you dwell) to be called places of prayer?** Explain.

_____
_____
_____
_____
_____
_____
_____
_____
_____
_____
_____
_____
_____

Session III. Unveiling the Power of Praise & Worship
(Read & Review *The Scribal Anointing*, pgs. 114-117)

1. **Praise and worship are _____ - not what you listen to or what you do. Explain.**

_____
_____
_____
_____
_____
_____
_____
_____
_____
_____
_____
_____

2. **Why should we embrace praise and worship as a lifestyle?**

_____
_____
_____

3. **How do we practice God's presence?** (Recall the things you do or the way you position yourself to get in Father's presence. For me, it begins by finding a quiet place in which I can pray undisturbed.)

_____
_____
_____
_____
_____

4. **What role does prayer play in praise and worship?**

_____
_____
_____
_____
_____
_____
_____
_____
_____

5. **Prayer, praise and worship are designed by God to work together in your life to bring breakthrough. Explain.**

_____
_____
_____
_____
_____
_____

6. **When true worship goes forth, the Lord often shows** _____.

7. **The priests or ministers under the old covenant were very selective about choosing praise and worshipers to go forth in the sanctuary. Why? How does this apply to us today being that "we" now represent the sanctuary of the Lord.** (1 Chronicles 15:22)

_____
_____
_____
_____
_____
_____

8. **Praise and worship went forth in the sanctuary and created an atmosphere for prophecy. How does this apply to us today?**

_____
_____
_____
_____
_____
_____

9. **The Lord reveals destiny in the midst of worship. What did He reveal to Joshua?** (Joshua 5:15)

_____
_____
_____
_____
_____
_____

Session IV. Unleashing The Scribal Anointing ® Within
(Read & Review *The Scribal Anointing*, pgs. 118-120)

1. **In David's worst times, how did approach the throne room of prayer and then enter into worship?** (Psalm 3:1-4 is an example.)

_____
_____
_____
_____
_____

2. **David knew how to press into Father's presence.** Have you pressed in to the Father's presence to this degree? If so, ask Holy Spirit to help you describe that experience.

_____

_____

_____

_____

_____

_____

3. **What was David's secret?** Looking through the Psalms, identify one in particular that shows Him in the midst of this process of entering in and then emerging restored.

_____

_____

_____

_____

_____

_____

_____

4. **What is journaling?**

_____

_____

_____

_____

_____

5. **How can journaling (or how has journaling) impacted your life?**

_____

_____

_____

_____

_____

_____

How does the Holy Spirit use journaling to bring healing in your life?

_____
_____
_____
_____
_____
_____
_____
_____
_____
_____
_____
_____
_____
_____

Made in the USA
San Bernardino, CA
04 April 2017